Heaven, Hell, and Life After Death

Kay Arthur, Bob & Diane Vereen

PRECEPT MINISTRIES INTERNATIONAL

WATERBROOK
PRESS

CONTENTS

How to Use This Study v

Introduction: Heaven, Hell, and Life After Death 1

Week One: Why Do We Have to Die? 3

Week Two: Can We Live Again After Death? 21

Week Three: What Can We Know About Resurrection? 37

Week Four: What Comes After Death for the Believer? 53

Week Five: What Comes After Death for the
Unrepentant? 77

Week Six: What Can We Know for Certain About
Heaven? 95

HOW TO USE THIS STUDY

This small-group study is for people who are interested in learning for themselves more about what the Bible says on various subjects, but who have only limited time to meet together. It's ideal, for example, for a lunch group at work, an early morning men's group, a young mothers' group meeting in a home, a Sunday-school class, or even family devotions. (It's also ideal for small groups that typically have longer meeting times—such as evening groups or Saturday morning groups—but want to devote only a portion of their time together to actual study, while reserving the rest for prayer, fellowship, or other activities.)

This book is designed so that all the group's participants will complete each lesson's study activities *at the same time*. Discussing your insights drawn from what God says about the subject reveals exciting, life-impacting truths.

Although it's a group study, you'll need a facilitator to lead the study and keep the discussion moving. (This person's function is *not* that of a lecturer or teacher. However, when this book is used in a Sunday-school class or similar setting, the teacher should feel free to lead more directly and to bring in other insights in addition to those provided in each week's lesson.)

If *you* are your group's facilitator, the leader, here are some helpful points for making your job easier:

- Go through the lesson and mark the text before you lead the group. This will give you increased familiarity with the material and will enable you to facilitate the discussion with greater ease. It may be easier for you to lead the group through the instructions for marking the text, if you, as a leader, choose a specific color for each symbol you mark.

- As you lead the group, start at the beginning of the text and simply read it aloud in the order it appears in the lesson, including the "insight boxes," which appear throughout. Work through the lesson together, observing and discussing what you learn. As you read the Scripture verses, have the group say aloud the word they are marking in the text.

- The discussion questions are there simply to help you cover the material. As the class moves into the discussion, many times you will find that they will cover the questions on their own. Remember, the discussion questions are there to guide the group through the topic, not to squelch discussion.

- Remember how important it is for people to verbalize their answers and discoveries. This greatly strengthens their personal understanding of each week's lesson. Try to ensure that everyone has plenty of opportunity to contribute to each week's discussions.

- Keep the discussion moving. This may mean spending more time on some parts of the study than on others. If necessary, you should feel free to spread out a lesson over more than one session. However, remember that you don't want to slow the pace too much. It's much better to leave everyone wanting more than to have people dropping out because of declining interest.

- If the validity or accuracy of some of the answers seems questionable, you can gently and cheerfully remind the group to stay focused on the truth of the Scriptures. Your object is to learn what the Bible says, not to engage in human philosophy. Simply stick with the Scriptures and give God the opportunity to speak. His Word *is* truth (John 17:17)!

HEAVEN, HELL, AND LIFE AFTER DEATH

We all know death is certain. Yet that certainty prompts many questions, such as, *Where is my loved one now? What is happening to him, to her? What about those who inflicted hell on my life—will they get what they deserve? And what awaits me on the other side of death?*

We want hope. Comfort. Assurance. We want answers.

Theories abound. Different religions offer varied scenarios from reincarnation to a paradise where sensual pleasures are fulfilled by virgins at our disposal. Some say there is a place called hell; others say a loving God would not condemn anyone to hell. Some say when you are dead, you are dead; that's the end. Others say it's just the beginning!

An abundance of books detail the experiences of

those who say they have died or had an out-of-body experience. Most describe a glorious scene that appeals to our imaginations. Others tell of torment. Which leaves us with even more questions:

- Can we trust the experiences of other human beings? What if they were deceived?
- Do we know heaven is for real only because someone went there and came back to tell us about it?
- Those surreal pictures of the afterlife bring either peace or consternation, but what if they are just imagination? *What if death is the end and nothing follows?*

With all these options, we can choose to believe what suits us. But wouldn't it be better to know the truth? To know what we can expect beyond death's door? What is right? What is true? What is certain? Surely if death comes to all, shouldn't we find out what happens after death?

Heaven, Hell, and Life After Death is a study designed to help you see for yourself what the Bible, the Word of God, has to say on the subject. Whatever you believe about the Bible, it will be well worth your time to discover what God Himself has to say on the subject. It might take the sting out of death!

Death is a reality. Sooner or later we will die. The Bible puts it this way in Psalm 89:48: "What man can live and not see death?"

Since death will touch us all, shouldn't we want to know the answers to questions like these:

- What is death?
- How does it come?
- Why do we all die?
- If God is love, why doesn't He stop it?

OBSERVE

Let's begin by looking at what the Bible says about the why of death and what comes after.

Leader: Read aloud Ecclesiastes 3:1–2 and Hebrews 9:27. Have the group say aloud and mark each key word as directed.

- *Circle each occurrence of* **appointed** *and* **time.**
- *Mark each occurrence of the word* **die** *with a tombstone symbol, like this:* ⌂

ECCLESIASTES 3:1–2

¹ There is an appointed time for everything. And there is a time for every event under heaven—

² A time to give birth and a time to die; a time to plant and a time to uproot what is planted.

HEBREWS 9:27

And inasmuch as it is appointed for men to die once and after this comes judgment.

As you read the text, it's helpful to have the group say the key words aloud as they mark them. This way everyone will be sure they are marking every occurrence of the word, including any synonymous words or phrases. Do this throughout the study.

DISCUSS

• What did you learn from marking *time* and *appointed* in these verses?

• According to Hebrews 9:27, what follows death, and what does this tell you about the person who dies? Is death the end of everything?

OBSERVE

In order to understand why man is appointed to die, we need to first have some understanding about life. Where did life come from?

Leader: Read aloud Genesis 2:7–9. Have the group say aloud and...

- *mark every reference to **the Lord God**, including pronouns, with a triangle, like this:* △
- *underline each reference to **man**, including the pronoun **his**.*
- *draw a squiggly line under the **two specific trees** mentioned, like this:* ∿∿

DISCUSS

- What did you learn about the Lord God in these verses?

- Although it may seem redundant, discuss what you learned from marking the references to man. When and how did man become a living being?

- What do these verses tell you about the relationship between the Lord God and man? What is one to the other?

- What two specific trees are mentioned in these verses?

7 Then the LORD God formed man of dust from the ground, and breathed into his nostrils the breath of life; and man became a living being.

8 The LORD God planted a garden toward the east, in Eden; and there He placed the man whom He had formed.

9 Out of the ground the LORD God caused to grow every tree that is pleasing to the sight and good for food; the tree of life also in the midst of the garden, and the tree of the knowledge of good and evil.

INSIGHT

According to Genesis 2:7, man was more than a physical being. God made the outer physical body out of "dust from the ground," and then He "breathed into his nostrils the breath of life." Simultaneously, at this breathing, "man became a living being," or as the King James Version says, "a living soul."

GENESIS 2:15–17

15 Then the LORD God took the man and put him into the garden of Eden to cultivate it and keep it.

16 The LORD God commanded the man, saying, "From any tree of the garden you may eat freely;

OBSERVE

Leader: Read aloud Genesis 2:15–17. Have the group…

- *underline each reference to **the man,** including the pronouns **him** and **you**.*
- *mark the word **die** with a tombstone:*

DISCUSS

- What did you learn from marking references to the man?

- Who's in control in this relationship, and how do you know?

17 but from the tree of the knowledge of good and evil you shall not eat, for in the day that you eat from it you will surely die."

- Is the man a mere puppet on a string, or does God give him a choice of whether or not to believe and obey? Explain your answer.

- What would be the consequence if the man disobeyed God?

• Of the two trees listed in Genesis 2:9, which specific one was Adam told not to eat from? Was he given any instruction regarding the other tree?

INSIGHT

Genesis 2:17 is the first time the word *die* is used in the Bible. In Hebrew, the language in which the Old Testament was written, *to die* means "to expire, to breathe out." It describes that point in time when man becomes absent from his physical body.

Physical death brings a separation of the body and soul. When the body expires and man breathes out the last breath of life, the body then returns to the ground, to dust (Genesis 3:19). Man dies physically, but his soul—the God-breathed part of his being—lives forever.

OBSERVE

According to the account of Genesis 2:18–25, God saw that it was not good for Adam to be alone, so He fashioned a woman out of one of his ribs to be a suitable helper for him.

Leader: Read Genesis 3:1–10 aloud. Have the group…

- *mark every reference to the serpent, including pronouns, with a pitchfork, like this:* ⚡
- *mark every reference to **God** with a triangle.*
- *underline every reference to **the woman**, **the husband**, including appropriate pronouns such as **you**, **we**, **they**, etc.*
- *put a tombstone over **die.***

DISCUSS

- Discuss the dialogue that took place between the serpent and the woman. What were the serpent's first words, and how did the woman answer?

GENESIS 3:1–10

1 Now the serpent was more crafty than any beast of the field which the LORD God had made. And he said to the woman, "Indeed, has God said, 'You shall not eat from any tree of the garden'?"

2 The woman said to the serpent, "From the fruit of the trees of the garden we may eat;

3 but from the fruit of the tree which is in the middle of the garden, God has said, 'You shall not eat from it or touch it, or you will die.'"

4 The serpent said to the woman, "You surely will not die!

5 "For God knows that in the day you eat from it your eyes will be opened, and you will be like God, knowing good and evil."

6 When the woman (saw) that the tree was good for food, and that it was a delight to the eyes, and that the tree was desirable to make one wise, she took from its fruit and ate; and she gave also to her husband with her, and he ate.

7 Then the eyes of both of them were opened, and they knew that they were naked; and they sewed fig leaves together and made themselves loin coverings.

• What was the serpent's perspective regarding the consequence for disobeying God? How did he reply when the woman told him why she couldn't eat from the tree of the knowledge of good and evil?

• Was the serpent telling the truth or a lie? Explain your answer.

• What did the woman do then? Circle the verbs that show each action that led up to eating the forbidden fruit. The first verb has been circled for you.

• Who else was involved in the woman's disobedience? How did that come about?

• What did they do immediately after their disobedience? What had changed to prompt this action on the part of Adam and Eve?

• Who went looking for whom?

• What insights can you gain into the results of disobedience from these verses? Discuss these.

8 They heard the sound of the LORD God walking in the garden in the cool of the day, and the man and his wife hid themselves from the presence of the LORD God among the trees of the garden.

9 Then the LORD God called to the man, and said to him, "Where are you?"

10 He said, "I heard the sound of You in the garden, and I was afraid because I was naked; so I hid myself."

REVELATION 12:9

And the great dragon was thrown down, the serpent of old who is called the devil and Satan, who deceives the whole world; he was thrown down to the earth, and his angels were thrown down with him.

JOHN 8:44

[Jesus is addressing men who claimed to be Abraham's descendants, but who were trying to kill Him.]

You are of your father the devil, and you want to do the desires of your father. He was a murderer from the beginning, and does not stand in the truth because there is no

OBSERVE

Let's look at two references that give us further insight into the serpent.

Leader: *Read Revelation 12:9 and John 8:44.*

> • *Have the group mark every reference to **the serpent, the devil,** including pronouns and synonyms, with a pitchfork.*

DISCUSS

• What did you learn about the serpent from these verses? Don't miss a thing! This is your enemy, and you need to know all God tells you about him.

• What truths do you see in these verses that relate to what you learned in Genesis? What is the nature of this enemy of man, the serpent, the devil?

OBSERVE

Now let's see what God said to Adam after he joined Eve in eating fruit from the tree of knowledge of good and evil.

Leader: Read Genesis 3:17–19. Have the group...
- *put a triangle over the pronouns **He** and **I** that refer to **God**.*
- *underline the references to **Adam**, including the pronoun **you**.*

DISCUSS

• What did you learn about Adam?

• Look at verse 17 again. What were Adam's options? Whose were the two voices Adam had to choose between? Think back to what you've observed in Genesis up to this point.

truth in him. Whenever he speaks a lie, he speaks from his own nature, for he is a liar and the father of lies.

GENESIS 3:17–19

17 Then to Adam He said, "Because you have listened to the voice of your wife, and have eaten from the tree about which I commanded you, saying, 'You shall not eat from it'; cursed is the ground because of you; in toil you will eat of it all the days of your life.

18 "Both thorns and thistles it shall grow for you; and you will eat the plants of the field;

19 By the sweat of your face you will eat bread, till you return to the ground, because from it you were taken; for you are dust, and to dust you shall return."

- Have you ever found yourself torn between obeying the commandments of God, as revealed in His Word, and listening to the word of another human being? Discuss briefly what made your decision difficult.

- What was Adam's punishment for his act of disobedience?

- Did Adam's punishment include physical death? How do you know from the text?

Genesis 3:20–24

20 Now the man called his wife's name Eve, because she was the mother of all the living.

21 The LORD God made garments of skin for Adam and his wife, and clothed them.

OBSERVE

The verdict for disobedience is that man is now destined to die, to return to dust. But is that all there is to the story? Thank heaven, it is not!

Leader: Read Genesis 3:20–24. Have the group...
- *put a triangle over every reference to **the Lord God**, including **Us**.*
- *underline each reference to **Adam** and **Eve**, including pronouns and synonyms.*

DISCUSS

• What did you learn about Eve from Genesis 3:20?

• So according to the Bible, the Word of God, who are the parents of all mankind? Or to put it another way, if you could trace the genealogy of all human beings, who would be the first parents?

• After Adam and Eve disobeyed God, they attempted to cover their nakedness with fig leaves. What did God do?

• What did God have to do to the animal in order to cover Adam and Eve's nakedness?

22 Then the LORD God said, "Behold, the man has become like one of Us, knowing good and evil; and now, he might stretch out his hand, and take also from the tree of life, and eat, and live forever"—

23 therefore the LORD God sent him out from the garden of Eden, to cultivate the ground from which he was taken.

24 So He drove the man out; and at the east of the garden of Eden He stationed the cherubim and the flaming sword which turned every direction to guard the way to the tree of life.

INSIGHT

If you stop to think about it, the first incident of physical death in the Word of God is that of an animal—the animal whose skin covered Adam and Eve's nakedness (Genesis 3:21). This is a beautiful picture, foreshadowing the later substitution of a blood sacrifice to cover the sin of mankind. In Leviticus 17:11 and Hebrews 9:22, God would explain that without the shedding of blood there is no atonement—no covering, no forgiveness—for sins. All of this points to the sacrifice of the Lamb of God, Jesus Christ, which alone can pay for our sins in full.

GENESIS 5:5

So all the days that Adam lived were nine hundred and thirty years, and he died.

OBSERVE

Leader: *Read Genesis 5:5 aloud. Have the group...*

- *underline the word **Adam** and the pronoun **he.***
- *put a tombstone over the word **died.***

DISCUSS

• What did you learn about Adam from this verse?

• How does Genesis 5:5 back up what God said in Genesis 2:17 would happen if Adam didn't obey Him?

• What does this tell you about God?

INSIGHT

From the beginning Adam had permission to eat from any tree of the garden, including the tree of life, except the tree of the knowledge of good and evil (Genesis 2:16–17). Adam had choices to make, and God was careful to tell him the consequences of his choices. If Adam had chosen to eat from the tree of life instead of the forbidden tree, he would have lived forever in fellowship with God. However, since Adam willfully chose to disobey, God in His mercy cast Adam and Eve from the garden to keep them from eating the fruit of the tree of life and living forever in a state of sin, separated from their Creator. As you will see, God in His omniscience had a Savior in the wings, the Lamb of God slain before the foundation of the world, who would come in "the fullness of time" (Galatians 4:4). Don't ever let the liar, the murderer, convince you that God doesn't love you or that He does not want the very best for you!

OBSERVE

Why didn't the consequence of death end with Adam and Eve?

Leader: Read Romans 5:12 aloud. Have the group...

- *mark **sin** and **sinned** with a big **S**.*
- *put a tombstone over each occurrence of the word **death**.*

ROMANS 5:12

Therefore, just as through one man sin entered into the world, and death through sin, and so death spread to all men, because all sinned.

DISCUSS

- How did sin and death enter into the world?

- Who was the "one man"? What was his wife's name, and what did it mean? If you don't remember, look at Genesis 3:20 again.

- What was the result of sin entering the world? For whom is this true? Does that include you?

WRAP IT UP

The decision that Adam and Eve made to disobey not only changed their lives but also reverberated down through history to affect every human being who has ever lived.

God has made it clear from the beginning: disobedience brings death. Because of Adam and Eve's sin, we all will one day experience a physical death. Dust shall return to dust.

As we saw in Ecclesiastes 3:1–2, each of us has an appointment with death, and we will keep the appointment no matter how busy we are, how inconvenient that moment is, how much is left undone. When God decides to repossess His breath of life, no last-minute buyout offer will be considered. We don't have the option to negotiate a longer time frame. God sets the date and time according to His schedule.

We also saw in Hebrews 9:27 that after death comes the judgment (see also 2 Timothy 4:1). What sort of judgment must we face? And is there a way of escape? Did this merciful, gracious, loving God who provided a covering for Adam and Eve's nakedness also provide a way forward for us?

Do we have any hope to live again after death? Next week, we'll see what God says.

We learned last week that each of us, without exception, has an appointment with death. But is death the end?

No! There is good news. Because God is a God of love and doesn't want any to perish, death can be a door that leads to eternal life.

Let's see for ourselves what God has to say in His Word, the Bible.

OBSERVE

As you saw last week, Adam and Eve chose to believe the serpent's lie and disobeyed the commandment of God. As a result they suffered the consequence of their sin, which was death.

Although we looked at Romans 5:12 last week, let's consider it again in the context of some other verses from Romans and see what more God says about sin and death.

Leader: *Read aloud Romans 3:9–10, 23; 5:12; and 6:23. Have the group say aloud and...*

- *mark every reference to **sin** with a big **S.***
- *put a tombstone over every occurrence of the word **death**, like this:* ⌂
- *draw a cloud like this* ⛅ *around the phrase **eternal life.***

ROMANS 3:9–10, 23

9 What then? Are we better than they? Not at all; for we have already charged that both Jews and Greeks are all under sin;

10 as it is written, "There is none right-eous, not even one."...

23 For all have sinned and fall short of the glory of God.

ROMANS 5:12

Therefore, just as through one man sin entered into the world, and death through sin, and so death spread to all men, because all sinned.

ROMANS 6:23

For the wages of sin is death, but the free gift of God is eternal life in Christ Jesus our Lord.

INSIGHT

In the days of the early church, using the phrase *Jews and Greeks* was like saying "Jews and Gentiles"; it's a reference to all mankind.

DISCUSS

• What did you learn from marking the references to sin?

• What did you learn from marking *death* in these verses?

• Keeping in mind what you observed last week in Genesis, who is the "one man" referred to in Romans 5:12 and what do you know about him?

• So according to the Word of God, what is the status of all mankind? Is there any possible way to overcome death? If so, what is it?

• What will it cost?

OBSERVE

Eternal life through Jesus Christ! A free gift! How is this possible?

Leader: Read aloud John 3:16–18, 36 and have the group...

- *draw a triangle, like this △ over every reference to **God**, including the pronouns **He** and **His**.*

- *mark every reference to **the Son**, or Jesus, including the pronoun **Him**, with a cross: ✝ Have the group say "Jesus" every time they mark a reference to Him.*

Leader: Read John 3:16–18, 36 again. This time have the group do the following:

- *Double underline every reference to **believe** and **obey**.*

- *For each reference to **not believing** or **not obeying**, put a slash like this ╱ over the word that is marked with a double underline.*

- *Draw a cloud ⌇⌇ around every occurrence of **eternal life** and **life**.*

JOHN 3:16–18, 36

16 For God so loved the world, that He gave His only begotten Son, that whoever believes in Him shall not perish, but have eternal life.

17 For God did not send the Son into the world to judge the world, but that the world might be saved through Him.

18 He who believes in Him is not judged; he who does not believe has been judged already, because he has not believed in the name of the only begotten Son of God....

36 He who believes in the Son has eternal

life; but he who does not obey the Son will not see life, but the wrath of God abides on him.

DISCUSS

• What do you learn about God from these verses?

• What do you learn about the Son? Don't miss a single detail!

• What does this passage say about believing, being saved, having eternal life?

• What would a person be saved from by believing in the Son of God?

• And what is true for the person who refuses to obey God's Son?

Luke 1:26–27, 30–35

26 Now in the sixth month the angel Gabriel was sent from God to a city in Galilee called Nazareth,

27 to a virgin engaged to a man whose name was Joseph, of the

OBSERVE

How did Jesus become the only begotten Son of God, and why is that important?

Leader: Read aloud Luke 1:26–27, 30–35 and Matthew 1:20–21. Have the group...
   • *underline every reference to **Mary**, including **virgin** and the pronouns **you** and **her**.*

• *put a cross* ✝ *over every reference to* **Jesus,** *watching carefully for all the pronouns and synonyms. Have the group say "Jesus" as they mark each reference.*

DISCUSS

• What did you learn about Mary from the text?

• How did Mary become pregnant with a son?

descendants of David; and the virgin's name was Mary.…

30 The angel said to her, "Do not be afraid, Mary; for you have found favor with God.

31 "And behold, you will conceive in your womb and bear a son, and you shall name Him Jesus.

32 "He will be great and will be called the Son of the Most High; and the Lord God will give Him the throne of His father David;

33 and He will reign over the house of Jacob forever, and His kingdom will have no end."

34 Mary said to the angel, "How can this be, since I am a virgin?"

35 The angel answered and said to her, "The Holy Spirit will come upon you, and the power of the Most High will over-shadow you; and for that reason the holy Child shall be called the Son of God."

MATTHEW 1:20–21

20 "Joseph, son of David, do not be afraid to take Mary as your wife; for the Child who has been conceived in her is of the Holy Spirit.

21 "She will bear a Son; and you shall call His name Jesus, for He will save His people from their sins."

• Whose son is it? Who is the father?

• What did you learn from marking the references to Jesus?

• Why was God's Son to be called Jesus?

• So was Jesus born with sin or without? Think: Who is His Father? How was Jesus conceived? Why was Jesus referred to as the "holy Child" (Luke 1:35)?

OBSERVE

Not only was Jesus born without sin, the Bible tells us that Jesus also never sinned, although He was "tempted in all things as we are" (Hebrews 4:15). Jesus always and only did what pleased the Father.

So why did Jesus leave heaven and become a human being like us? Let's see what God's Word says.

Leader: Read Hebrews 2:9, 14–15 and 2 Corinthians 5:21 slowly. Have the group…
- *put a cross over every reference to **Jesus,** including the pronouns **He, Himself,** and **Him.***
- *underline every reference to **mankind,** such as the synonyms and pronouns **everyone, children, those, our,** and **we.***

Leader: Read the text again. This time have the group…
- *mark with a tombstone every occurrence of the word **death.***
- *mark every reference to the **devil,** including pronouns, with a pitchfork.*

HEBREWS 2:9, 14–15

⁹ But we do see Him who was made for a little while lower than the angels, namely, Jesus, because of the suffering of death crowned with glory and honor, so that by the grace of God He might taste death for everyone.…

¹⁴ Therefore, since the children share in flesh and blood, He Himself likewise also partook of the same, that through death He might render powerless him who had the power of death, that is, the devil,

¹⁵ and might free those who through

fear of death were subject to slavery all their lives.

2 CORINTHIANS 5:21

He [God] made Him [Jesus] who knew no sin to be sin on our behalf, so that we might become the righteousness of God in Him.

DISCUSS

• What did you learn from marking the pronouns that refer to Jesus?

• What did you learn from marking the references to mankind?

• What does it mean that Jesus shared in "flesh and blood," and why is this important?

• What did you learn from marking *death*?

• Stop and think: What gives the devil the power of death? (Remember Romans 6:23: "the wages of sin is death.")

• If Jesus paid for your sins in full by becoming sin for you, what has happened to the devil's power? Why?

• What kind of news is this, and why?

OBSERVE

Perhaps you've heard of "the gospel." What does this term mean? The gospel is the good news about Jesus Christ, who can give us salvation through the forgiveness of our sins. The apostle Paul laid out the fundamentals of the gospel for us in chapter 15 of his letter to the Corinthians, in what has come to be called the resurrection chapter.

Let's look at a portion of it, along with 1 John 2:2.

Leader: *Read 1 Corinthians 15:1–7 and 1 John 2:2 aloud. Have the group do the following:*

- *Place a check mark like this ✔ over every reference to the **gospel,** including the pronoun **which** and the phrase **the word which I preached to you.***
- *Circle every **that,** beginning in verse 3.*
- *Put a cross over every reference to **Christ,** including the pronouns **He** and **Himself.***

1 CORINTHIANS 15:1–7

1 Now I make known to you, brethren, the gospel which I preached to you, which also you received, in which also you stand,

2 by which also you are saved, if you hold fast the word which I preached to you, unless you believed in vain.

3 For I delivered to you as of first importance what I also received, that Christ died for our sins according to the Scriptures,

4 and that He was buried, and that He was raised on the third day according to the Scriptures,

5 and that He appeared to Cephas, then to the twelve.

6 After that He appeared to more than five hundred brethren at one time, most of whom remain until now, but some have fallen asleep;

7 then He appeared to James, then to all the apostles.

1 JOHN 2:2

He Himself is the propitiation for our sins; and not for ours only, but also for those of the whole world.

Leader: Now read 1 Corinthians 15:1–7 and 1 John 2:2 aloud again. This time have the group do the following:
- *Put a tombstone over the word died.*
- *Mark the word raised with an upward arrow, like this:↑*

DISCUSS

• What did you learn from marking all the references to the gospel in verses 1 and 2?

• Is it enough to simply hear the gospel, to be able to explain it to another person? Is anything else required? What do you learn from verses 1 and 2?

• What do you think it means to believe "in vain"?

• So what are we to believe? What was the gospel message that was delivered in verses 3–7? Look at the *that*s you circled and you will see essentials of the gospel that are to be believed and not deviated from. Discuss them and then answer the following:

• Why did Jesus die, and what does this require a believer to admit about himself or herself?

• What does the fact that Jesus was buried tell you?

• What happened after Jesus was buried?

• Since Jesus died, was buried, and rose from the dead, what can you know about His death for mankind's sin? Was it sufficient to pay the debt of sin for every human being? (Look again at 1 John 2:2.)

INSIGHT

Propitiation means "satisfaction." Jesus' death satisfied the holiness of a righteous God; therefore God could forgive the sin of all mankind. But this payment applies only for those who accept it, who believe in the good news that Jesus Christ died for our sins and, having satisfied the righteousness of His holy Father, rose from the dead never to die again. Sin was paid for and therefore death was conquered.

The main points of the gospel are these:

1. Jesus died for our sins according to the Scriptures. The proof of His death is His burial.

2. Jesus rose from the dead according to the Scriptures. The proof of His resurrection was the fact that Jesus was seen by numerous people on varying occasions.

Together, the death of Jesus Christ and His bodily resurrection guarantee that our sins are forgiven in full and there will be a resurrection to life for all who believe, who hold fast to this gospel. This is good news!

OBSERVE

Let's wrap up this week's study with a passage that further confirms the certainty of life after physical death for those who truly believe Jesus is the Christ, the Son of God.

Leader: Read 1 Corinthians 15:20–22 aloud. Have the group do the following:

- *Put a cross over every reference to Christ (Jesus), including synonyms and pronouns. As you mark each reference, have the group say "Jesus" aloud.*
- *Put a tombstone over every reference to death.*
- *Mark raised, resurrection, made alive with an upward arrow.*

1 CORINTHIANS 15:20–22

20 But now Christ has been raised from the dead, the first fruits of those who are asleep.

21 For since by a man came death, by a man also came the resurrection of the dead.

22 For as in Adam all die, so also in Christ all will be made alive.

DISCUSS

• What did you learn from marking the references to Christ?

• What did you learn from marking the references to death?

• Who is the man by whom death came, and why did it come? (Keep in mind what you learned last week in Genesis.)

• What does it mean to be in Christ versus in Adam? What's the destination of those in Adam? And of those who are in Christ?

• So where are you—in Adam or in Christ? How do you know?

WRAP IT UP

Every second, people die. Twenty-four hours a day, seven days a week. Try as we might to sustain life, death is inevitable because we are all born in sin.

However, there is good news—wondrous news, life-changing news. Our Creator loves us. He did not abandon us in our sin; rather, He loved us, even before we turned to Him (1 John 4:19). It is written in His Word and preserved for eternity: "While we were yet sinners, Christ died for us.… While we were enemies we were reconciled to God through the death of His Son" (Romans 5:8, 10).

There is life beyond death's door for all who will believe Jesus is the Son of God, the sinless One who paid for our sins in full and thereby broke Satan's power of death.

"And the testimony is this, that God has given us eternal life, and this life is in His Son. He who has the Son has the life; he who does not have the Son of God does not have the life" (1 John 5:11–12).

So let's ask the question again, since the answer is a matter of eternal life or eternal death: What awaits you beyond death's door—and how do you know?

So far in our study we have seen that death is certain—and why. However, God is about life, not death. In His love, mercy, and omniscience God provided a way of escape. From the beginning, in multiple ways we don't have time to explore fully in this study, God let man know that the Messiah, the Christ, would come. In the fullness of time God would send His Son, born of a virgin, born without sin, so that He might pay our debt of sin in full, offering us forgiveness of sins and the gift of eternal life. This Anointed One would crush the head of the serpent of old (Genesis 3:15).

So what do we need to know about life after death? What can we learn about the raising of the dead? What happens after death for those who believe in Jesus Christ and for those who do not? And who determines the time of death?

This is what we want to look at this week.

OBSERVE

Let's take the last question first: Who determines the time of death? Can an individual postpone death or choose the day of death?

Leader: *Read aloud Ecclesiastes 8:8 and Matthew 6:27. As you do, have the group say aloud and...*

- *underline every reference to **man**, including the pronoun **you**.*

ECCLESIASTES 8:8

No man has authority to restrain the wind with the wind, or authority over the day of death.

MATTHEW 6:27

And who of you by
being worried can add
a single hour to his
life?

• *circle every reference to* **time,** *words like* **day** *and* **hour.**

• *mark the word* **death** *with a tomb-stone:* ⌂

DISCUSS

• After a person gets over the shock of hearing that he or she has a condition that will result in death, what generally becomes that individual's goal?

• What did you learn from marking the words *man* and *you*?

• What kind of feelings does this knowledge provoke, and why?

OBSERVE

If no man has authority over the day of his death, who or what governs life and death?

Leader: Read aloud Job 14:5 and Psalm 139:16. Have the group...
  • *underline the references to* **man: his, he, my, me.**
  • *put a triangle over the pronouns* **You** *and* **Your,** *which here refer to* **God.**

DISCUSS

• Taking one verse at a time, discuss what you learn from marking *man* and *God* in these verses.

• So who determines how long a person lives?

• What questions does this knowledge bring to your mind? How does this make you feel?

• If a person doesn't believe in God, does this change who determines how long that individual will live? Explain your answer.

JOB 14:5

Since his days are determined, the number of his months is with You; and his limits You have set so that he cannot pass.

PSALM 139:16

Your eyes have seen my unformed substance; and in Your book were all written the days that were ordained for me, when as yet there was not one of them.

DEUTERONOMY 32:39

See now that I, I am He, and there is no god besides Me; it is I who put to death and give life. I have wounded and it is I who heal, and there is no one who can deliver from My hand.

1 SAMUEL 2:6

The LORD kills and makes alive; He brings down to Sheol and raises up.

REVELATION 1:17–18

[The Him is Jesus Christ. The year is approximately AD 90, about sixty years after Jesus' crucifixion. The one writing is John, one of the twelve apostles chosen by Jesus.]

OBSERVE

Leader: *Read aloud Deuteronomy 32:39; 1 Samuel 2:6; and Revelation 1:17–18. Have the group say aloud and mark…*

- *every reference to **God**, including pronouns, with a triangle.*
- *every reference to **death** and **kill** with a tombstone.*
- *each reference to **Jesus** (in the verses from Revelation) with a cross.*

INSIGHT

Sheol is a difficult word to translate. However, when you look at how it is used in the Bible, it is always connected with death, with the grave. The Septuagint, the Greek translation of the Old Testament, translated the Hebrew *Sheol* as *Hades,* meaning "the unseen."

DISCUSS

• What did you learn from marking the references to God in Deuteronomy and 1 Samuel? Don't miss a single truth!

• What did you learn from marking the references to Jesus in the verses from Revelation? Watch closely so you don't miss anything.

• What did you learn about death? What does it mean that Jesus "holds the keys of death and Hades"? Stop and think: What do keys do?

• If you have lost a loved one, how does knowing that God is in charge of death make you feel? Why?

17 When I saw Him, I fell at His feet like a dead man. And He placed His right hand on me, saying, "Do not be afraid; I am the first and the last,

18 and the living One; and I was dead, and behold, I am alive forevermore, and I have the keys of death and of Hades."

JOB 14:14

If a man dies, will he live again? All the days of my struggle I will wait until my change comes.

JOB 19:25-27

25 As for me, I know that my Redeemer lives, and at the last He will take His stand on the earth.

26 Even after my skin is destroyed, yet from my flesh I shall see God;

27 Whom I myself shall behold, and whom my eyes will see and not another.

OBSERVE

The book of Job is the oldest book of the Bible. In it Job asked a question that is on the heart of multitudes.

Leader: Read Job 14:14 and 19:25–27 aloud. Have the group...

- *draw a squiggly line under **the question Job asks,** like this:* ﹏﹏
- *underline the references to **Job,** watching for the pronouns **me, I,** and **my.***
- *put a cross over every reference to **Redeemer,** including pronouns.*

DISCUSS

- What question did Job ask, and what conclusion did he come to?

- What did you learn from marking the references to Job?

- What did you learn from marking the references to *Redeemer?*

• What did you read in these verses that indicates Job believed in a resurrection of the body?

OBSERVE

Let's look at two other Old Testament scriptures that speak of a resurrection.

Leader: Read aloud Isaiah 26:19 and Daniel 12:2 and have the group...
   • *put a tombstone over **dead, corpses, lie in the dust, departed spirits,** and **sleep.***
   • *draw a cloud* {☁} *over the words **awake** and **life**.*

DISCUSS

• What did you learn from marking all the references to death?

• What terms are used that suggest these verses describe a resurrection of the dead?

• What are the two destinations of "those who sleep"?

ISAIAH 26:19

Your dead will live; their corpses will rise. You who lie in the dust, awake and shout for joy, for your dew is as the dew of the dawn, and the earth will give birth to the departed spirits.

DANIEL 12:2

Many of those who sleep in the dust of the ground will awake, these to everlasting life, but the others to disgrace and everlasting contempt.

MATTHEW 22:23–24, 28–32

23 On that day some Sadducees (who say there is no resurrection) came to Jesus and questioned Him,

24 asking, "Teacher, Moses said, 'If a man dies having no children, his brother as next of kin shall marry his wife, and raise up children for his brother.'…

28 "In the resurrection, therefore, whose wife of the seven will she be? For they all had married her."

29 But Jesus answered and said to them, "You are mistaken, not understanding the Scriptures nor the power of God.

OBSERVE

In the time of Jesus, did everyone who claimed to worship God believe in a resurrection? What did Jesus teach?

Let's look at two passages from the Gospels. We will begin with a passage in Matthew, where a religious group of Jews questioned Jesus on the resurrection. They presented an example where seven brothers died, one after another without producing an heir. In accordance with the Law, each in turn married the same woman, who remained childless through all seven marriages. Then the wife died.

Leader: Read Matthew 22:23–24, 28–32 aloud. Have the group do the following:

- *Mark every reference to **death** with a tombstone.*
- *Draw an upward arrow over each occurrence of the word **resurrection.***
- *Put a slash through the phrase **no resurrection.***
- *Mark the references to **God** with a triangle.*

DISCUSS

• What did you learn from marking the references to *resurrection*?

• What did you learn about God in these verses?

• How does Jesus' response support the certainty of the resurrection?

30 "For in the resurrection they neither marry nor are given in marriage, but are like angels in heaven.

31 "But regarding the resurrection of the dead, have you not read what was spoken to you by God:

32 'I am the God of Abraham, and the God of Isaac, and the God of Jacob'? He is not the God of the dead but of the living."

JOHN 11:11–15

11 This He [Jesus] said, and after that He said to them, "Our friend Lazarus has fallen asleep; but I go, so that I may awaken him out of sleep."

12 The disciples then said to Him, "Lord, if he has fallen asleep, he will recover."

13 Now Jesus had spoken of his death, but they thought that He was speaking of literal sleep.

14 So Jesus then said to them plainly, "Lazarus is dead,

15 and I am glad for your sakes that I was not there, so that you may believe; but let us go to him."

OBSERVE

Near the end of His final year of ministry, Jesus received word that Lazarus, a dear friend, was sick. Yet instead of going to his side immediately, Jesus delayed traveling to see him for two days.

Leader: Read John 11:11–15. Have the group do the following:

- *Underline the references to **Lazarus**, including pronouns.*
- *Put a semicircle over **sleep, fallen asleep**, like this:* ⌒
- *Put a tombstone over the words **death** and **dead.***
- *Double underline the word **believe.***

DISCUSS

- What did you learn about Lazarus?

- What did you learn from marking *fallen asleep*? What did Jesus mean by that?

- What was one purpose of Jesus' delay?

Leader: Read John 11:17, 21–26 aloud. Have the group do the following:

- *Underline all the references to **Lazarus**, including synonyms and pronouns.*
- *Mark all references to **death** with a tombstone.*
- *Put an upward arrow over every occurrence of **rise again** and **resurrection**.*
- *Put a cloud around **life, live,** and **lives**.*
- *Double underline each occurrence of **believe(s)**.*

DISCUSS

- What did you learn about Lazarus in these verses?

- What did Martha believe about resurrection?

- What did you learn from marking the references to rising again, the resurrection?

JOHN 11:17, 21–26

17 So when Jesus came, He found that he had already been in the tomb four days....

21 Martha then said to Jesus, "Lord, if You had been here, my brother would not have died.

22 "Even now I know that whatever You ask of God, God will give You."

23 Jesus said to her, "Your brother will rise again."

24 Martha said to Him, "I know that he will rise again in the resurrection on the last day."

25 Jesus said to her, "I am the resurrection and the life; he who

believes in Me will live even if he dies,

26 and everyone who lives and believes in Me will never die. Do you believe this?"

- What did you learn about how one can live even if he dies?

- For whom is this possible? What did you learn from marking *believe(s)*?

JOHN 5:24–29

[Jesus is speaking.]

24 Truly, truly, I say to you, he who hears My word, and believes Him who sent Me, has eternal life, and does not come into judgment, but has passed out of death into life.

25 Truly, truly, I say to you, an hour is coming and now is, when the dead will

OBSERVE

Let's see what Jesus taught about the resurrection before this incident with Lazarus.

Leader: Read John 5:24–29. Have the group mark the following:
- *every pronoun referring to **Jesus**— every **I, My,** and **Me**—with a cross.*
- *each occurrence of **eternal life, life,** and **live** with a cloud.*
- *all references to **death, dead** with a tombstone.*
- *every occurrence of the word **resurrection** with an upward arrow.*

DISCUSS

• What did you learn about Jesus in this passage of Scripture?

• What is true of those who hear His word and believe in God?

• What will happen when the dead hear the voice of the Son of God?

• What did Jesus teach about the resurrection? What two distinctions did He draw?

Leader: *Give the group members time to think about the following question.*

• If the resurrection were to happen today, which group would you be in? How do you know?

hear the voice of the Son of God, and those who hear will live.

26 For just as the Father has life in Himself, even so He gave to the Son also to have life in Himself;

27 and He gave Him authority to execute judgment, because He is the Son of Man.

28 Do not marvel at this; for an hour is coming, in which all who are in the tombs will hear His voice,

29 and will come forth; those who did the good deeds to a resurrection of life, those who committed the evil deeds to a resurrection of judgment.

EPHESIANS 1:13–14

¹³ In Him [Jesus], you also, after listening to the message of truth, the gospel of your salvation—having also believed, you were sealed in Him with the Holy Spirit of promise,

¹⁴ who is given as a pledge of our inheritance, with a view to the redemption of God's own possession, to the praise of His glory.

ROMANS 8:10–11, 23

¹⁰ If Christ is in you, though the body is dead because of sin, yet the spirit is alive because of righteousness.

¹¹ But if the Spirit of Him who raised Jesus

OBSERVE

Finally, let's look at the role of the Holy Spirit in respect to the resurrection of those who die as believers.

Leader: Read Ephesians 1:13–14 and Romans 8:10–11, 23. Have the group do the following:

- *Underline the pronouns you, your, we, and our.*
- *Mark the references to the Spirit of God, including pronouns, like this:*
- *Over every reference to body or bodies, including the phrase God's own possession, draw a stick figure:*

DISCUSS

- What is the progression of events in the believer's life, as described by Paul in Ephesians 1:13–14?

- What do these two passages teach about our bodies?

- Where in these verses do you see a division, a separation, between the body and the spirit of a human being? Is this division permanent? Explain your answer.

- From all you've learned so far in this study, do you think we will be recognizable as individuals after death, as we are today? Will we recognize those we've known before death? What makes you think as you do?

- Review what these verses teach about the Holy Spirit. Don't miss a detail!

from the dead dwells in you, He who raised Christ Jesus from the dead will also give life to your mortal bodies through His Spirit who dwells in you....

23 And not only this, but also we ourselves, having the first fruits of the Spirit, even we ourselves groan within ourselves, waiting eagerly for our adoption as sons, the redemption of our body.

WRAP IT UP

The death of a loved one can bring such pain. So much so that we don't want to hear, or even think, that God had anything to do with their death. Yet when you get a full biblical understanding of God, of His character and sovereignty, knowing and embracing the truths you've been learning can bring great comfort and a peace that passes understanding.

No human being can die, or even commit suicide, unless God allows it to happen. Because God is sovereign, He rules over all, including death and the day of death. The resurrection of Jesus takes the pain, the agony, out of death. Death could not hold Him (Acts 2:24)! He was "delivered over because of our transgressions, and was raised because of our justification" (Romans 4:25). We have hope if, or because, we have a savior named Jesus!

As you consider this, beloved of God, remember that God is love—and much more. He is holy, righteous, and perfect in all His ways. God can never act apart from the totality of who He is; therefore, everything that comes into our lives is filtered through His fingers of love. While we may have questions, while we may wonder with whys and hows and even twinges of doubt, peace comes only when we decide to embrace and cling to what God tells us in His Word, the Bible.

So consider what you've learned these past three weeks. Remember, the grave is not the end. There is a resurrection—a resurrection of the righteous to life and a resurrection of the wicked to eternal judgment.

Next week we will take a closer look at the resurrection to life, which ought to encourage you greatly, especially if you or a loved one is facing the news of impending death.

A comprehensive study of the whole of Scripture indicates that within every human body is a soul, the spirit of man, which lives on after the body dies. The question is, where does that soul go after physical death?

What comes after death for believers? Will we get new bodies? If so, when? And what will they be like?

This week we'll consider all these questions as we learn what the Bible reveals about what lies beyond death's door for the child of God.

OBSERVE

Leader: *Read James 2:26 and Matthew 10:28. Have the group say aloud and…*

- *mark each occurrence of **body** with a stick figure like this:* ☿
- *draw a squiggly line under **soul** and **spirit**, like this:* ∿∿∿
- *put a triangle over **Him**, which refers here to **God the Father**.*

DISCUSS

- What did you learn from marking the references to the body?

- What did you learn from marking *spirit* and *soul?*

JAMES 2:26

For just as the body without the spirit is dead, so also faith without works is dead.

MATTHEW 10:28

[Jesus is speaking.]

Do not fear those who kill the body but are unable to kill the soul; but rather fear Him who is able to destroy both soul and body in hell.

• Jesus' disciples were going to be hated by the world and consequently they would suffer greatly, some to the point of death. How might Jesus' words in Matthew 10:28 have helped them?

• The word *fear* carries the idea of respect, trust. When it comes to understanding death, who are you going to believe? From what you've learned, can any human being take your life without God's permission? So who are you to fear?

LUKE 16:19–26

19 Now there was a rich man, and he habitually dressed in purple and fine linen, joyously living in splendor every day.

20 And a poor man named Lazarus was laid at his gate, covered with sores,

OBSERVE

If death involves the separation of soul from body, what happens to the soul, the spirit of a man, after his body dies? Let's see what we can learn from the account Jesus gave of the lives and deaths of two men— and their encounter with Abraham of old.

Leader: Read Luke 16:19–26 aloud. Have the group do the following:

• Mark the reference to the **rich man** with a dollar sign, like this: **$**

- *Underline all references to the **poor man**, who is named **Lazarus**.*
- *Put a tombstone over **died.***
- *Mark **Hades** with a downward arrow, like this:* ↓

DISCUSS

- What do you learn about the rich man's life before he died?

- What do you learn about the poor man's life before he died?

- What happened to the rich man after he died? Where was he, and what was it like?

INSIGHT

Hades is the Greek term for the realm of the dead, the dwelling of the wicked. It is the holding place of unbelievers from the time of their death until their final judgment, which we will study in week 5.

21 and longing to be fed with the crumbs which were falling from the rich man's table; besides, even the dogs were coming and licking his sores.

22 Now the poor man died and was carried away by the angels to Abraham's bosom; and the rich man also died and was buried.

23 In Hades he lifted up his eyes, being in torment, and saw Abraham far away and Lazarus in his bosom.

24 And he cried out and said, "Father Abraham, have mercy on me, and send Lazarus so that he may dip the tip of his finger in water and cool off

my tongue, for I am in agony in this flame."

25 But Abraham said, "Child, remember that during your life you received your good things, and likewise Lazarus bad things; but now he is being comforted here, and you are in agony.

26 "And besides all this, between us and you there is a great chasm fixed, so that those who wish to come over from here to you will not be able, and that none may cross over from there to us."

• Compare Lazarus with the rich man. What was Lazarus's situation after death?

• Abraham mentioned "a great chasm" in verse 26. Consider where each soul is in this account. What does this tell you about death?

• From all you've studied in God's Word, what happens after death? Is there any reversal, or changing, of destinations? Explain your answer.

OBSERVE

Let's look at the rest of the story.

Leader: Read aloud Luke 16:27–31. Have the group:

- *Mark each reference to the **rich man** and **Lazarus,** including pronouns, with a stick figure.*
- *Draw a downward arrow to mark **place of torment.***
- *Put a tombstone over each occurrence of the word **dead.***

INSIGHT

"Moses and the Prophets" is a reference to the Jewish Bible, the Old Testament. There was no New Testament at the time of Jesus' life and ministry.

DISCUSS

- What did the rich man request in these verses, and why?

- What concern prompted his request, according to verse 28?

LUKE 16:27–31

27 And he [the rich man] said, "Then I beg you, father, that you send him to my father's house—

28 for I have five brothers—in order that he may warn them, so that they will not also come to this place of torment."

29 But Abraham said, "They have Moses and the Prophets; let them hear them."

30 But he said, "No, father Abraham, but if someone goes to them from the dead, they will repent!"

31 But he said to him, "If they do not listen to Moses and the Prophets, they will not be persuaded even if someone rises from the dead."

• What was Abraham's reply to the rich man's request? Don't just repeat it; discuss what Abraham said. Think of the magnitude of his words, the truth he declared.

• Read verses 30–31 again. *Repent* means "to have a change of mind that leads to a change of direction." What did the rich man think would make his brothers repent? What does this tell you about the rich man's brothers?

• How did Abraham reply to the rich man?

• Remember, we saw in week 2 that Jesus died and rose again according to the Scriptures; those Scriptures were the Old Testament—"Moses and the Prophets." So how important is the Old Testament portion of the Bible to you?

OBSERVE

Does the passage we just read describe the *final* destination of the soul? Are we ultimately destined for either the torment of Hades or the comfort of Abraham's bosom? Or is the resurrection of the body still to come? Let's look again at Paul's resurrection chapter, which we touched on in week 2, to see what it says.

Leader: Read 1 Corinthians 15:12–22 aloud. Have the group say and mark...

- *every reference to **Christ**, including pronouns, with a cross.*
- *every reference to **resurrection**, including the synonyms **raised** and **made alive**, with an upward arrow.*
- *each occurrence of **dead** and **fallen asleep** with a tombstone.*
- *every reference to **God**, including pronouns, with a triangle.*

Leader: Read it again slowly so the group can absorb what the text teaches us.

1 CORINTHIANS 15:12–22

12 Now if Christ is preached, that He has been raised from the dead, how do some among you say that there is no resurrection of the dead?

13 But if there is no resurrection of the dead, not even Christ has been raised;

14 and if Christ has not been raised, then our preaching is vain, your faith also is vain.

15 Moreover we are even found to be false witnesses of God, because we testified against God that He raised Christ, whom He did not raise, if in fact the dead are not raised.

16 For if the dead are not raised, not even Christ has been raised;

17 and if Christ has not been raised, your faith is worthless; you are still in your sins.

18 Then those also who have fallen asleep in Christ have perished.

19 If we have hoped in Christ in this life only, we are of all men most to be pitied.

20 But now Christ has been raised from the dead, the first fruits of those who are asleep.

21 For since by a man came death, by a man also came the resurrection of the dead.

DISCUSS

• What are the implications of saying there is no resurrection, of believing that everything ends for an individual with the tomb, the coffin, the ashes?

• If there is no resurrection, what are the consequences, according to:

Verse 17?

Verse 18?

Verse 19?

• In verse 20, what does the phrase "first fruits" mean and what does it point to?

• So according to verses 20–22, is there a resurrection of those who are referred to as being asleep? If so, how—through whom—is it possible?

22 For as in Adam all die, so also in Christ all will be made alive.

OBSERVE

Since we live on after death, what kind of bodies will we have? Let's see what the apostle Paul went on to tell the Corinthians.

Leader: Read aloud 1 Corinthians 15: 35–38. Have the group...
  • *mark **dead** and **dies** with a tombstone.*
  • *put an upward arrow over **raised** and **come to life.***
  • *draw a stick figure over every occurrence of **body** when referring to the body of a human soul.*

DISCUSS

• What questions are raised in verse 35, and how did Paul respond?

• What did you learn from marking the references to the body?

1 CORINTHIANS 15:35–38

35 But someone will say, "How are the dead raised? And with what kind of body do they come?"

36 You fool! That which you sow does not come to life unless it dies;

37 and that which you sow, you do not sow the body which is to be, but a bare grain, perhaps of wheat or of something else.

38 But God gives it a body just as He wished, and to each of the seeds a body of its own.

• What does this imply about our resurrected bodies?

• Who determines what they will be like?

• So who raises the dead?

---

1 CORINTHIANS 15:42–49

42 So also is the resurrection of the dead. It is sown a perishable body, it is raised an imperishable body;

43 it is sown in dishonor, it is raised in glory; it is sown in weakness, it is raised in power;

44 it is sown a natural body, it is raised a spiritual body. If there is a natural body, there is also a spiritual body.

OBSERVE

There's more to learn from this chapter. Paul isn't finished yet!

Leader: Read 1 Corinthians 15:42–49 aloud. Have the group do the following:

• *Put an upward arrow over each occurrence of* **resurrection** *and* **raised.**

• *Draw a stick figure over every reference to* **the body,** *including the pronoun* **it.**

• *Although He is not mentioned by name, put a cross over anything you think refers to* **Jesus.**

• *Mark the words* **spiritual, heaven,** *and* **heavenly** *with a cloud.*

DISCUSS

• What did you learn about the resurrected body in verses 42–44?

• What contrasts are made in verses 45–49? Read each verse carefully so you don't miss a thing.

• Who is the first Adam? The last Adam?

• Which comes first—the natural or the spiritual? What point was Paul making with this comparison?

45 So also it is written, "The first man, Adam, became a living soul." The last Adam became a life-giving spirit.

46 However, the spiritual is not first, but the natural; then the spiritual.

47 The first man is from the earth, earthy; the second man is from heaven.

48 As is the earthy, so also are those who are earthy; and as is the heavenly, so also are those who are heavenly.

49 Just as we have borne the image of the earthy, we will also bear the image of the heavenly.

LUKE 24:35–43

35 They began to relate their experiences on the road and how He was recognized by them in the breaking of the bread.

36 While they were telling these things, He Himself stood in their midst and said to them, "Peace be to you."

37 But they were startled and frightened and thought that they were seeing a spirit.

38 And He said to them, "Why are you troubled, and why do doubts arise in your hearts?

39 "See My hands and My feet, that it is

OBSERVE

If we will bear the image of Jesus, the "second man" from heaven, what will our resurrected bodies be like? Let's listen in on a conversation between two men and Jesus after His resurrection to see what we can learn about His resurrected body.

Leader: Read Luke 24:35–43 aloud. Have the group...

- *underline every pronoun referring to **the men**—every **they** and **them**.*
- *circle everything that you learn about **Jesus' resurrected body**.*

DISCUSS

- What did you learn about the resurrected Jesus? What was He like? What did He do?

• What does verse 39 say about "a spirit"?

• What insight does this give you about *your* resurrected body?

I Myself; touch Me and see, for a spirit does not have flesh and bones as you see that I have."

40 And when He had said this, He showed them His hands and His feet.

41 While they still could not believe it because of their joy and amazement, He said to them, "Have you anything here to eat?"

42 They gave Him a piece of a broiled fish;

43 and He took it and ate it before them.

2 CORINTHIANS 5:1–8

¹ For we know that if the earthly tent which is our house is torn down, we have a building from God, a house not made with hands, eternal in the heavens.

² For indeed in this house we groan, longing to be clothed with our dwelling from heaven,

³ inasmuch as we, having put it on, will not be found naked.

⁴ For indeed while we are in this tent, we groan, being burdened, because we do not want to be unclothed but to be clothed, so that what is mortal will be swallowed up by life.

OBSERVE

You've observed what Paul wrote about the resurrection in 1 Corinthians 15. He had even more to say to the Christians at Corinth in his letter known as 2 Corinthians.

Leader: *Read 2 Corinthians 5:1–8 aloud, slowly. Have the group simply listen as you read the text. Then read it slowly a second time and have the group…*

- *underline every pronoun that refers to* ***believers****—every* ***we, our,*** *and* ***us.***
- *mark every reference to our* ***earthly tent*** *—including synonyms such as our* ***house*** *and* ***at home****—with a tent, like this:* ∧

Leader: *Read the text a third time and have the group…*

- *put a tombstone over the phrases* ***torn down*** *and* ***absent from the body.***
- *mark with a cloud every reference to the* ***house not made with hands, our dwelling from heaven.*** *Watch carefully for pronouns.*

DISCUSS

• What did you learn about the "tent," the house we live in now? How does it compare to the "house not made with hands"?

• What was Paul saying in verse 4? What did he mean by "unclothed"?

• What have we received as a pledge, a guarantee, that we will get immortal bodies?

• Do you remember seeing a reference to this guarantee in scriptures we studied earlier?

• What did Paul say about death, about being absent from the body as a believer?

• How do most people you know view death, and why do you think this is?

• If their perspective is different from what God teaches, do you believe you have any responsibility to these people? Why or why not?

5 Now He who prepared us for this very purpose is God, who gave to us the Spirit as a pledge.

6 Therefore, being always of good courage, and knowing that while we are at home in the body we are absent from the Lord—

7 for we walk by faith, not by sight—

8 we are of good courage, I say, and prefer rather to be absent from the body and to be at home with the Lord.

1 CORINTHIANS 15:50–54

50 Now I say this, brethren, that flesh and blood cannot inherit the kingdom of God; nor does the perishable inherit the imperishable.

51 Behold, I tell you a mystery; we will not all sleep, but we will all be changed,

52 in a moment, in the twinkling of an eye, at the last trumpet; for the trumpet will sound, and the dead will be raised imperishable, and we will be changed.

53 For this perishable must put on the imperishable, and this mortal must put on immortality.

OBSERVE

Why do we need new bodies? And what if we are alive when Jesus comes?

Leader: Read 1 Corinthians 15:50–54 aloud. Have the group do the following:
- *Underline each occurrence of **flesh and blood, perishable,** and **mortal.***
- *Circle every reference to **imperishable** and **immortality.***
- *Put a tombstone over the words **sleep, dead,** and **death.***

INSIGHT

A *mystery* is a truth that up to this point hasn't been revealed.

Sleep, as you saw with Jesus' friend, Lazarus, is a term used for the physical death of a believer.

DISCUSS

- What did you learn from marking *flesh and blood, perishable,* and *mortal*?

• What is the mystery Paul revealed?

• When Paul wrote that we will not all sleep, what was he saying?

• So what are the two possible states, or conditions, of believers before we are changed?

• What does it mean that "we will all be changed"? According to verses 52–54, what will happen and how?

OBSERVE

First Thessalonians gives us further insight into the mystery Paul revealed in 1 Corinthians 15:50–54. Let's see what we can learn.

Leader: Read 1 Thessalonians 4:13–18. Have the group...

- • *put a cross over every reference to **Jesus,** including pronouns and synonyms such as **the Lord.***
- • *circle every reference to **those who are asleep, the dead in Christ.** Watch carefully for pronouns and synonyms.*

54 But when this perishable will have put on the imperishable, and this mortal will have put on immortality, then will come about the saying that is written, "Death is swallowed up in victory."

1 THESSALONIANS 4:13–18

13 But we do not want you to be uninformed, brethren, about those who are asleep, so that you will not grieve as do the rest who have no hope.

14 For if we believe that Jesus died and rose again, even so God will bring with

Him [Jesus] those who have fallen asleep in Jesus.

15 For this we say to you by the word of the Lord, that we who are alive and remain until the coming of the Lord, will not precede those who have fallen asleep.

16 For the Lord Himself will descend from heaven with a shout, with the voice of the archangel and with the trumpet of God, and the dead in Christ will rise first.

17 Then we who are alive and remain will be caught up together with them in the clouds to meet the Lord in the air, and so

DISCUSS

• What did you learn from marking the references to those who have fallen asleep? Move through the text verse by verse.

• What do you learn from marking the references to Jesus? Put a cloud around anything that tells you about His coming.

• Remember that in 2 Corinthians 5:8 you saw that when a believer dies he or she is present with the Lord in heaven. According to these verses in 1 Thessalonians, where are those who have fallen asleep, in respect to the Lord?

• What happens to a believer who falls asleep? Look at the drawing below.

Believer Immediately Absent from Body, Present with Lord

Heaven

Earth

Believer's Body (Fallen Asleep)

Saved and Alive

Living but Lost

we shall always be with the Lord.

18 Therefore comfort one another with these words.

OBSERVE

Leader: Read 1 Thessalonians 4:13–18 aloud again. This time have the group…

> • *underline every reference to the living, including we and brethren.*

DISCUSS

• What did you learn about those who are alive when Jesus comes? What happens to them?

• Discuss what you see on the following diagram.

1 Thessalonians 4:13-18

*4:14
Dead
in Christ*

Heaven

*Lord's Coming
to Meet Us
in the Air*

4:14, 16

4:17

4:16   *Earth*

*Alive,   Living
Changed,   but Lost
Raising   Leaving to
of Body   Meet Lord
of Believer   in the Air
Who Is in
Heaven*

• How does the timing of this compare with what's happening for those who are asleep?

• What do you think about all this?

OBSERVE

So what should be a believer's perspective about life and death? Let's see what the apostle Paul wrote when he was being held as a prisoner in Rome because of the gospel.

Leader: Read Philippians 1:21–24 aloud. Have the group…

• *underline every reference to **Paul**— each **me** and **I**.*

• *put a tombstone over **die, depart**.*

21 For to me, to live is Christ and to die is gain.

22 But if I am to live on in the flesh, this will mean fruitful labor for me; and I do not know which to choose.

23 But I am hard-pressed from both directions, having the desire to depart and be with Christ, for that is very much better;

24 yet to remain on in the flesh is more necessary for your sake.

DISCUSS

• What did you learn from marking the references to Paul?

• What was Paul's dilemma? Why did he feel torn?

• How did Paul look at death?

• So what does this tell you about life after death for the believer?

• Do you personally think of dying as gaining? Why or why not?

WRAP IT UP

Death is hard, isn't it? The separation seems so permanent. Your loved one is gone. No more talking, seeing, touching. Your life has changed, and it's difficult to adjust to the gaping hole that person's absence has created.

But as you have seen, though out of reach, that person still exists. And if your loved one was a believer, death is not the end. He or she is present with the Lord. Not unclothed, not a disembodied, unrecognizable spirit, but the person who lived once in a mortal body. And one day you will be together again if you both were true believers! Your separation from your saved loved one is temporal.

As we studied in 1 Thessalonians, we who truly trust in Jesus Christ don't grieve over death as others who have no hope. Although it is hard to imagine, difficult to grasp in all its fullness, God's Word tells us that to die is gain, for the new dwelling of the believer's soul will be far better!

And so we wait eagerly for the redemption of our own bodies. A resurrection is coming. Mortal will put on immortality. Death will be swallowed up in victory. You will be reunited with your loved one. You will live forever and ever with your God.

Doesn't knowing this make you eager to share the good news of Jesus Christ with others so that they too might believe and receive the life that is ours in Christ? Why would we be ashamed of the gospel, hesitant to present it, if it is the power of God to salvation (Romans 1:16)? If believing the gospel brings the guarantee of life after death, a life far better than anything we'll know here?

As you read previously in John 5, Jesus told of a time when those in the tombs would hear God's voice and come forth either to a resurrection of life or to a resurrection of judgment.

In the early fourteenth century, the poet Dante wrote his description of the awful and final judgment that awaits the dead. Michelangelo in turn painted his interpretation of this event on the walls of the Sistine Chapel in Rome. As you stand in the chapel trying to take it all in, you can almost hear the screams of the grotesque figures suffering in the agony of eternal fire.

But what does God Himself tell us about the destiny of those who die apart from Jesus Christ? What will happen at the resurrection of those human beings who loved darkness rather than light, those who would not come to Jesus, the light of the world, the light of life, that their deeds might be seen for what they were? What awaits the souls who refused to seek and receive the mercy and forgiveness of God found only in God's Son, the Lord Jesus Christ?

What will their resurrection be like?

OBSERVE

When the apostle Paul arrived in Athens and found himself surrounded by idols, his spirit was greatly grieved. Let's listen in on his conversation with the worshipers of these idols and see what we can learn that will help us better understand the destiny of those who do not worship the one and only true God and His Son.

Acts 17:22–28, 30–31

22 So Paul stood in the midst of the Areopagus and said, "Men of Athens, I observe that you are very religious in all respects.

23 "For while I was passing through and examining the objects of your worship, I also found an altar with this inscription, 'To an unknown god.' Therefore what you worship in ignorance, this I proclaim to you.

24 "The God who made the world and all things in it, since He is Lord of heaven and earth, does not dwell in temples made with hands;

Leader: Read Acts 17:22–28, 30–31. Have the group do the following:

- *Underline every reference to the **men of Athens,** including pronouns.*
- *Mark every reference to **God,** including synonyms and pronouns, with a triangle.*
- *Circle the words **times** and **day.***
- *Put a cross over the words **Man** and **Him** when they refer to **Jesus.***

DISCUSS

- What insights did you gain from marking the references to the men of Athens in verses 22–23?

- What did Paul tell these men about God? Look at all the references to God that you marked.

- According to verse 30, what is God declaring to all men everywhere? Why?

INSIGHT

The Greek word translated in Acts 17:30 as *repent* means "to have a change of mind"—a change that affects what you believe, the way you behave, and therefore alters the direction of your life.

---

25 nor is He served by human hands, as though He needed anything, since He Himself gives to all people life and breath and all things;

26 and He made from one man every nation of mankind to live on all the face of the earth, having determined their appointed times and the boundaries of their habitation,

27 that they would seek God, if perhaps they might grope for Him and find Him, though He is not far from each one of us;

28 for in Him we live and move and exist....

30 "Therefore having overlooked the times of ignorance, God is now declaring to men that all people everywhere should repent,

31 because He has fixed a day in which He will judge the world in righteousness through a Man whom He has appointed, having furnished proof to all men by raising Him from the dead."

• What did you learn from marking the references to Jesus in verse 31?

HEBREWS 9:27

And inasmuch as it is appointed for men to die once and after this comes judgment.

OBSERVE

In our first week of study, we looked at Hebrews 9:27. Let's look at it again.

Leader: *Have the group read Hebrews 9:27 aloud. Then read it again and have the group...*
   • *circle the phrases referring to **time**— **once** and **after**.*
   • *mark **judgment** with a big **J**.*

DISCUSS

- What does this verse teach you about death? Don't miss a single point, as there is more than one.

OBSERVE

When we are judged, we want justice—unless of course we are guilty. Then we beg for mercy. So who is the Judge, and how will He judge?

Leader: Read aloud Psalm 9:7–8; Psalm 96:12–13; and Matthew 16:27. Have the group…

- *underline every reference to **the Lord,** including the pronouns **He** and **Him** and the synonym **Son of Man**. (We are underlining because **Lord** can refer to either the Father or the Son.)*
- *put a cloud around any reference to **the Lord's coming.***

PSALM 9:7–8

7 But the LORD abides forever; He has established His throne for judgment,

8 And He will judge the world in righteousness; He will execute judgment for the peoples with equity.

PSALM 96:12–13

12 Let the field exult, and all that is in it. Then all the

trees of the forest will
sing for joy

13 before the LORD,
for He is coming, for
He is coming to
judge the earth. He
will judge the world
in righteousness and
the peoples in His
faithfulness.

MATTHEW 16:27

For the Son of Man is
going to come in the
glory of His Father
with His angels, and
will then repay every
man according to his
deeds.

DISCUSS

• What did you learn from marking the
references to the Lord?

• According to Matthew 16:27, on what
basis does God repay every man? Does
that seem fair?

• From all you've learned these past weeks,
does this mean we are saved by our deeds,
or does it mean that our deeds show what
we believe? Explain your answer.

INSIGHT

What is the relationship between faith and deeds?

Ephesians 2:8–10 tells us we are saved by God's grace alone, apart from our works, our deeds. Deeds are a product of what we believe. The book of Titus tells us that Jesus "gave Himself for us to redeem us from every lawless deed, and to purify for Himself a people for His own possession, zealous for good deeds" (2:14). Our faith is not proved or demonstrated simply by what we profess, but by how we live. When Paul wrote Titus, he warned him about those who professed to know God but by their deeds denied Him (Titus 1:16).

JOHN 5:21–22, 28–29

[Jesus is speaking.]

21 For just as the Father raises the dead and gives them life, even so the Son also gives life to whom He wishes.

22 For not even the Father judges anyone, but He has given all judgment to the Son....

28 Do not marvel at this; for an hour is coming, in which all who are in the tombs will hear His voice,

29 and will come forth; those who did the good deeds to a resurrection of life, those who committed the evil deeds to a resurrection of judgment.

OBSERVE

In week 3 we considered two of the following verses from John 5 from the aspect of resurrection. Now let's review them from the perspective of judgment to learn what Jesus taught on this subject.

Leader: Read John 5:21–22, 28–29 aloud. Have the group…

- *put a cross over every reference to **the Son,** including pronouns.*
- *mark every reference to **judges, judgment** with a big **J.***
- *mark each occurrence of the word **deeds** with a big **D.***

DISCUSS

- What did you learn from marking the references to the Son?

- What kinds of deeds are mentioned in these verses, and what is the result of each?

OBSERVE

Both John the Baptist and Jesus Himself warned of the punishment that would come to the disobedient who refused to believe the words of Jesus. Let's take a quick look at two of these warnings.

Leader: Read Matthew 3:10–12 and Mark 9:43, 47–48. Have the group do the following:
- *Mark every reference to **fire** with flames, like this:* 〰
- *Put a cross over every **He** and **His** that refers to **Jesus**.*
- *Mark the word **hell** with a big **H**.*

INSIGHT

The Greek word translated here as "hell" is *Gehenna,* and it refers specifically to the final destination of the unrepentant. (*Hades,* also translated as "hell," means something different, as we will shortly see.) Gehenna was also the name of a valley in Jerusalem where the trash of the city burned continuously.

MATTHEW 3:10–12

[John is speaking.]

10 The axe is already laid at the root of the trees; therefore every tree that does not bear good fruit is cut down and thrown into the fire.

11 As for me, I baptize you with water for repentance, but He who is coming after me is mightier than I, and I am not fit to remove His sandals; He will baptize you with the Holy Spirit and fire.

12 His winnowing fork is in His hand, and He will thoroughly clear His threshing floor; and He will gather His

wheat into the barn, but He will burn up the chaff with unquenchable fire.

MARK 9:43, 47–48

[Jesus is speaking.]

43 If your hand causes you to stumble, cut it off; it is better for you to enter life crippled, than, having your two hands, to go into hell, into the unquenchable fire....

47 If your eye causes you to stumble, throw it out; it is better for you to enter the kingdom of God with one eye, than, having two eyes, to be cast into hell,

48 where their worm does not die, and the fire is not quenched.

DISCUSS

• What did you learn from marking the references to Jesus?

• What about the fire? Who or what experiences it? Take it verse by verse from the text.

• What did you learn about hell?

• What was Jesus teaching about the hand and eye in Mark 9? What point was He trying to get across?

OBSERVE

Let's look at the final words of Isaiah, the prophet to the nation of Israel, speaking on behalf of God. The context of his prophecy is the time when all the nations will come to see God's glory. This will happen during Messiah's reign on the earth, when He rules the nations with a rod of iron.

Leader: Read Isaiah 66:22–24 aloud. Have the group...

- *put a triangle over every pronoun referring to **the Lord,** whose words are being prophesied by Isaiah.*
- *underline every reference to **all mankind,** including pronouns, beginning with verse 23.*

Leader: Read the text again. This time have the group...

- *put a tombstone over every reference to the **corpses,** including pronouns.*
- *mark **fire** like this:* ⋀⋁⋀

ISAIAH 66:22–24

22 "For just as the new heavens and the new earth which I make will endure before Me," declares the LORD, "so your offspring and your name will endure.

23 "And it shall be from new moon to new moon and from sabbath to sabbath, all mankind will come to bow down before Me," says the LORD.

24 "Then they will go forth and look on the corpses of the men who have transgressed against Me. For their worm will not die and their fire will not be quenched; and they will be an abhorrence to all mankind."

DISCUSS

• What did you learn about the Lord from these verses?

• Summarize what God is saying. What will "all mankind" do and when?

• Why do you suppose they look on the "corpses of the men?" What lesson might this make visible to them?

• What did you learn from marking *fire*? Who experiences it and for how long?

REVELATION 20:11–15

11 Then I saw a great white throne and Him who sat upon it, from whose presence earth and heaven fled away,

OBSERVE

When we studied the account of the rich man and Lazarus last week, we saw that the rich man was in torment in Hades. But was Hades his final destination? Let's see what God teaches us in the last book of the Bible.

Leader: *Read Revelation 20:11–15 aloud. Have the group…*

- *mark the references to **the throne**, including pronouns, with a big* **T.**
- *put a tombstone over every reference to **the dead**, including pronouns.*

Leader: *Read Revelation 20:11–15 aloud again. This time have the group…*

- *mark the phrase **lake of fire** with circle upon circle, like this:* ⊚
- *mark every reference to **deeds** with a big* **D.**
- *draw a box around each occurrence of **book(s)**, like this:* ☐

Leader: *Now have the group read the entire passage aloud together. Do it slowly so they can absorb what they are reading.*

DISCUSS

Leader: *The answers to the following questions may overlap; however, because of the gravity of this passage, we suggest you have the group answer each one so nothing is missed. These are truths that bear repeating.*

and no place was found for them.

12 And I saw the dead, the great and the small, standing before the throne, and books were opened; and another book was opened, which is the book of life; and the dead were judged from the things which were written in the books, according to their deeds.

13 And the sea gave up the dead which were in it, and death and Hades gave up the dead which were in them; and they were judged, every one of them according to their deeds.

14 Then death and Hades were thrown

into the lake of fire. This is the second death, the lake of fire.

15 And if anyone's name was not found written in the book of life, he was thrown into the lake of fire.

• What did you learn from marking *throne*? Whose throne is it?

• What did you learn from marking *the dead*?

• What did you learn from marking *deeds*? How does this compare with Jesus' warning in Mark 9 about our eyes and our hands?

• What did you learn from marking *books*? How are they described?

• What did you learn from marking *lake of fire*?

• Why do you think this is referred to as "the second death"?

• From all you've learned these past weeks, do those who refuse to believe in Jesus Christ ever experience true life?

INSIGHT

Why might the lake of fire be called "the second death"? Let's reason together. Ephesians 2:1 says we were all dead in our trespasses and sins— we are born sinners and "the wages of sin is death" (Romans 6:23).

Life is only ours when Jesus Christ is ours. Therefore, could it be referred to as a second death because these people never "passed out of death into life" (John 5:24) by believing on Jesus Christ? Because they never possessed Jesus Christ, in whom alone there is life? In John 14:6 Jesus said He is the way, the truth, and the life. So those who never received Jesus are twice dead—physically and spiritually. They never experienced life. They never will! How horribly sad, how eternally tragic.

• What book does your name have to be in
  if you are going to escape the lake of fire?

• In the light of the reality of the eternal
  punishment that awaits every human
  being who does not believe in Jesus Christ
  as evidenced by their deeds, what do you
  think is your responsibility?

• From what you have studied up to this
  point, do you have any idea how long the
  lake of fire lasts?

WRAP IT UP

So what happens to an unbeliever when he or she dies? It is obvious from all we've studied in God's Word that the soul of any person—saved or lost—does not cease to exist. As we saw in our study of Luke 16, although separated from his physical body, the rich man still experienced the pain of the flames and torment of Hades. He could see Lazarus in the bosom of Abraham. He was conscious as he requested the aid of Lazarus; the dead man's tongue needed water! Although separate from his physical body, he still had his faculties.

As you saw this week, when Jesus admonished His listeners in Mark 9 to do whatever was necessary to stop sinning with their hands and eyes, He warned them that if their bodies were cast into hell, they would experience a fire that would not end!

So often when a person well known to society dies, there is mention of them being in a better place or even being in heaven. However, whether the individual was great or small, if he or she did not believe on Jesus Christ, confess Him before others as Lord and Savior, and live a life that bore the fruit of faith, it's a delusion to claim that individual went to a better place—it's a lie that glosses over the certainty of death and the judgment that follows.

In Matthew 25:31–46, in Jesus' account of the separation of the sheep and the goats and their consequent destiny, our Lord makes it clear that the lake of fire was prepared not for man but for the devil and his angels. Yet those human beings who choose to believe the father of lies, rather than obeying the Son of God, will share in Satan's destiny: the lake of fire. They "will go away into eternal punishment, but the righteous into eternal life" (Matthew 25:46). Note that Jesus, the One who is the truth, tells us both are eternal!

No wonder the prophet Amos said, "Prepare to meet your God" (Amos 4:12). Are *you* prepared? And are you encouraging others to prepare?

While last week's study was heavy, our final week ought to bring sweet relief, for we're going to focus on heaven. This, beloved, is what eternity can hold for you: life. Life beyond death's door!

OBSERVE

Let's begin our study by looking at several verses that give us insight into heaven.

Leader: Read aloud Isaiah 66:1–2; Matthew 6:9–10; and Psalm 16:11.

- *Have the group put a triangle over every reference to **the Lord**. Watch carefully for pronouns and synonyms such as **Father**.*

DISCUSS

- What did you learn from marking the references to the Lord?

ISAIAH 66:1–2

¹ Thus says the LORD, "Heaven is My throne and the earth is My footstool. Where then is a house you could build for Me? And where is a place that I may rest?

² "For My hand made all these things, thus all these things came into being," declares the LORD.

MATTHEW 6:9–10

[Jesus is speaking to His disciples.]

⁹ Pray, then, in this way: "Our Father who

is in heaven, hallowed be Your name.

10 "Your kingdom come. Your will be done, on earth as it is in heaven."

PSALM 16:11

You will make known to me the path of life; in Your presence is fullness of joy; in Your right hand there are pleasures forever.

JOHN 14:1–6

1 "Do not let your heart be troubled; believe in God, believe also in Me.

2 "In My Father's house are many dwelling places; if it were not so, I would have told you; for I go to prepare a place for you.

• What specifically did you learn about heaven?

OBSERVE

As Jesus celebrated His final Passover with His disciples, He told them He was about to be betrayed and that He was going away. Sensing their troubled hearts, He offered the reassuring words you're about to read.

Leader: Read John 14:1–6 aloud. Have the group...

• *mark every reference to **Jesus** with a cross.*

• *put a box around every reference to **place(s)**, including **where** and **there**.*

DISCUSS

• What did you learn about Jesus in these verses?

• What did you learn from marking the references to place? List any details the text gives you about the place where Jesus was going.

• Discuss the sequence of events laid out by Jesus in respect to His going and coming. Note how His disciples are involved.

• How does anyone get access to the Father and His house?

• So, according to Jesus, is there any other way?

• What does that tell you about other religions?

³ "If I go and prepare a place for you, I will come again and receive you to Myself, that where I am, there you may be also.

⁴ "And you know the way where I am going."

⁵ Thomas said to Him, "Lord, we do not know where You are going, how do we know the way?"

⁶ Jesus said to him, "I am the way, and the truth, and the life; no one comes to the Father but through Me."

ACTS 1:9–11

9 And after He had said these things, He was lifted up while they were looking on, and a cloud received Him out of their sight.

10 And as they were gazing intently into the sky while He was going, behold, two men in white clothing stood beside them.

11 They also said, "Men of Galilee, why do you stand looking into the sky? This Jesus, who has been taken up from you into heaven, will come in just the same way as you have watched Him go into heaven."

OBSERVE

Let's look next at some verses that tell us what happened the final time the apostles saw the resurrected Jesus—and that reveal where Jesus is now, today!

Leader: *Read aloud Acts 1:9–11 and Romans 8:34. Have the group…*

- *put a cross over every reference to **Jesus,** including pronouns.*
- *underline every reference to **the apostles.** Don't miss a single pronoun.*

DISCUSS

- What do you learn about Jesus in these texts?

- According to what you learned in Acts, how did Jesus get where He is? Will He remain there permanently?

- According to Romans 8, what is Jesus doing?

• And according to what you saw previously in John 14, what else is Jesus doing?

• What does this reveal about you as a believer?

ROMANS 8:34
Christ Jesus is He who died, yes, rather who was raised, who is at the right hand of God, who also intercedes for us.

OBSERVE

Before we proceed any further today, let's review some events we've studied, along with other related facts, and put them in chronological order. This will help us better understand what we'll learn next about heaven.

• In the fullness of time, Jesus became flesh and blood, born of a virgin, born without sin. He was tempted as we are, but He never sinned.

• Jesus was crucified, made sin for us, died, and was buried.

• On the third day Jesus rose from the dead. He was seen multiple times by numerous people, all of whom could testify to His resurrection.

• Forty days after Jesus' resurrection He ascended into heaven to prepare a place for us who are believers in Jesus Christ.

- The Holy Spirit was then given to everyone who would believe in Jesus Christ. The Spirit is the guarantee of a believer's entrance into heaven at death and the redemption of the body.
- When a believer in Christ dies, he or she is absent from the body and present with the Lord.
- At some future point in time, Jesus will leave heaven, bringing with Him the souls of all believers who physically died before His return. Each of our souls will be reunited with a resurrected, immortal, imperishable body like the body of Jesus Christ (1 Thessalonians 4:13–18; 1 Corinthians 15:51–54).
- When Jesus returns to earth, He will subdue the nations. "The kingdom of the world has become the kingdom of our Lord and of His Christ; and He will reign forever and ever" (Revelation 11:15).
- Revelation 20:1–7 tells us that Jesus will reign for one thousand years. At the end of that time, the devil will

be cast "into the lake of fire and brimstone, where…[he] will be tormented day and night forever and ever" (Revelation 20:10).

• The unsaved dead of all the ages will then stand before the Great White Throne of God. The unbelieving dead—along with death and Hades—will be cast into the lake of fire (Revelation 20:11–15).

• Then there will be a new heaven and new earth (Revelation 21–22).

Since heaven is our subject, let's see what we can learn about our new home and what life will be like there for the true believer in Jesus, the Messiah.

Leader: Read Revelation 21:1–7 aloud. Have the group do the following:

• *Mark the word **heaven** with a cloud.*

• *Put a triangle over every reference to **God,** including pronouns.*

• *Put a box around every reference to **the holy city,** including synonyms like **New Jerusalem** and **tabernacle of God.***

REVELATION 21:1–7

1 Then I saw a new heaven and a new earth; for the first heaven and the first earth passed away, and there is no longer any sea.

2 And I saw the holy city, new Jerusalem, coming down out of heaven from God, made ready as a bride adorned for her husband.

3 And I heard a loud voice from the throne, saying, "Behold, the tabernacle of God is among men, and He will dwell among them, and they shall be His people, and God Himself will be among them,

4 and He will wipe away every tear from their eyes; and there will no longer be any death; there will no longer be any mourning, or crying, or pain; the first things have passed away."

DISCUSS

• What did you learn about the holy city in these verses?

• What did you learn about God? Describe His relationship to His people.

• What did you learn about the people of God, including their relationship with God Himself?

5 And He who sits on the throne said, "Behold, I am making all things new." And He said, "Write, for these words are faithful and true."

6 Then He said to me, "It is done. I am the Alpha and the Omega, the beginning and the end. I will give to the one who thirsts from the spring of the water of life without cost.

7 "He who overcomes will inherit these things, and I will be his God and he will be My son."

REVELATION 21:8

But for the cowardly and unbelieving and abominable and murderers and immoral persons and sorcerers and idolaters and all liars, their part will be in the lake that burns with fire and brimstone, which is the second death.

OBSERVE

The description you just read of the believer's future stands in stark contrast to what follows in the next verse.

Leader: Read Revelation 21:8 aloud. Have the group do the following:

- *Underline every reference to the individuals described in this verse.*
- *Mark the lake that burns with fire and brimstone with overlapping circles:* ◎
- *Put a tombstone over death, marking it with a big 2.*

DISCUSS

- Discuss the individuals listed in this verse and their lifestyles. What is their destination?

- What does this tell you about heaven?

OBSERVE

Leader: Read the selected verses from Revelation 21 aloud. Have the group...

- *Put a cross over every reference to **the Lamb**.*
- *Draw a large box around every reference to **the city**, including the pronouns **it** and **its**.*
- *Mark every reference to **God** with a triangle.*

DISCUSS

- What does this passage tell you about the holy city?

- What does this passage tell you about the Lamb and God?

REVELATION 21:9–10, 22–23, 27

9 Then one of the seven angels who had the seven bowls full of the seven last plagues came and spoke with me, saying, "Come here, I will show you the bride, the wife of the Lamb."

10 And he carried me away in the Spirit to a great and high mountain, and showed me the holy city, Jerusalem, coming down out of heaven from God....

22 I saw no temple in it, for the Lord God the Almighty and the Lamb are its temple.

23 And the city has no need of the sun or of the moon to shine

on it, for the glory of God has illumined it, and its lamp is the Lamb....

27 and nothing unclean, and no one who practices abomination and lying, shall ever come into it, but only those whose names are written in the Lamb's book of life.

• Who can live in this city?

• Does this describe you? If so, how can these truths help you handle life today?

OBSERVE

Leader: Read aloud Revelation 22:1–6, which provides a further description of the New Jerusalem. Have the group…

- *mark **the throne** with a big* **T.**
- *mark **the tree of life** with a tree, like this:*
- *place a big* **X** *over the word **curse.***
- *underline every reference to **bond-servants**, including pronouns.*

DISCUSS

- Describe the picture given to us in this final chapter of God's Word. What are we left with as God brings His revelation to a close?

- Now, look at the details. What do you learn about the tree? What is it called? What is it for?

1 Then he showed me a river of the water of life, clear as crystal, coming from the throne of God and of the Lamb,

2 in the middle of its street. On either side of the river was the tree of life, bearing twelve kinds of fruit, yielding its fruit every month; and the leaves of the tree were for the healing of the nations.

3 There will no longer be any curse; and the throne of God and of the Lamb will be in it, and His bond-servants will serve Him;

4 they will see His face, and His

name will be on their foreheads.

5 And there will no longer be any night; and they will not have need of the light of a lamp nor the light of the sun, because the Lord God will illumine them; and they will reign forever and ever.

6 And he said to me, "These words are faithful and true"; and the Lord, the God of the spirits of the prophets, sent His angel to show to His bond-servants the things which must soon take place.

- What did you learn about this tree in Genesis 3:22 in week 1 of this study (see page 15)?

- What did you learn from marking *curse* in Revelation 22:3?

- Discuss this in light of the curse brought upon mankind through the sin of Adam and Eve. Compare this with what you read earlier this week in Revelation 21:4.

- Are you a bond-servant of Jesus Christ? If so, what does this text tell you about your future?

OBSERVE

Let's close our study with the following words from our Father's book.

Leader: *Read aloud 1 Peter 1:3–5; Luke 10:20; and Philippians 3:20.*
- *Have the group underline every pronoun referring to* **believers—our, us, you, who, your,** *and* **we.**

DISCUSS

- What did you learn from marking the references to those who are "born again to a living hope," those who have believed that Jesus is the Christ, the Son of God? What is true for those whose deeds prove their relationship is real?

1 PETER 1:3–5

3 Blessed be the God and Father of our Lord Jesus Christ, who according to His great mercy has caused us to be born again to a living hope through the resurrection of Jesus Christ from the dead,

4 to obtain an inheritance which is imperishable and undefiled and will not fade away, reserved in heaven for you,

5 who are protected by the power of God through faith for a salvation ready to be revealed in the last time.

LUKE 10:20

Rejoice that your names are recorded in heaven.

PHILIPPIANS 3:20

For our citizenship is in heaven, from which also we eagerly wait for a Savior, the Lord Jesus Christ.

• Discuss what these truths mean to you personally.

WRAP IT UP

Even so, come quickly Lord Jesus!

Oh what a glorious day that will be

when we see Jesus face to face,

when we feel the touch of God's hand as He Himself wipes
away our tears.

When all sorrow, all pain will be gone.

No more tears.

And no more darkness!

Sin and death will have been conquered—

never to plague us again.

Finally we will be able to worship and serve our God and Father
with undistracted devotion.

This is heaven. *This is life!*

This is eternal life,
that they may know You, the only true God,
and Jesus Christ whom you have sent.

John 17:3

4️⃣0️⃣ No-Homework
MINUTE
BIBLE
STUDIES # Bible Studies

That Help You Discover Truth For Yourself

Being a Disciple:
Counting the Real Cost

Kay Arthur, Tom & Jane Hart

Having a Real
Relationship
With God

Kay Arthur

How Do You
Walk the Walk
You Talk?

Kay Arthur

Living a
Life of
True Worship

Kay Arthur, Bob & Diane Vereen

Living
Victoriously in
Difficult Times

Kay Arthur, Bob & Diane Vereen

How to Make
Choices You
Won't Regret

Kay Arthur, David & BJ Lawson

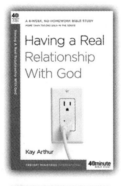
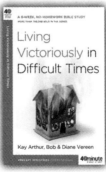

Also Available:

A Man's Strategy for
    Conquering Temptation
Rising to the Call of Leadership
Key Principles of Biblical Fasting
What Does the Bible Say About Sex?
Turning Your Heart Toward God

Fatal Distractions: Conquering
    Destructive Temptations
Spiritual Warfare: Overcoming the Enemy
The Power of Knowing God
Breaking Free from Fear
Finding Hope After Divorce

Another powerful study series from beloved Bible teacher

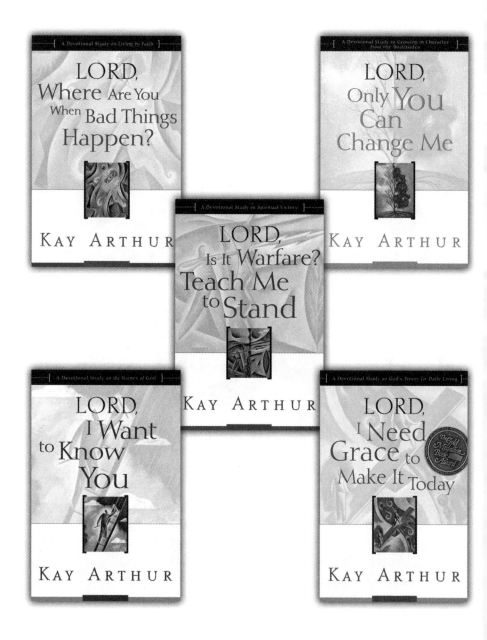

{ A Devotional Study on Living by Faith }

LORD, Where Are You When Bad Things Happen?

KAY ARTHUR

{ A Devotional Study on Growing in Character from the Beatitudes }

LORD, Only You Can Change Me

KAY ARTHUR

{ A Devotional Study on Spiritual Victory }

LORD, Is It Warfare? Teach Me to Stand

KAY ARTHUR

{ A Devotional Study on the Names of God }

LORD, I Want to Know You

KAY ARTHUR

{ A Devotional Study on God's Power for Daily Living }

LORD, I Need Grace to Make It Today

KAY ARTHUR

KAY ARTHUR

The Lord series provides insightful, warm–hearted Bible studies designed to meet you where you are—and help you discover God's answers to your deepest needs.

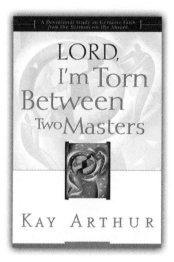

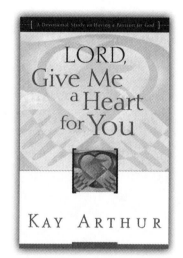

ALSO AVAILABLE:
One–year devotionals to draw you closer to the heart of God.

ABOUT KAY ARTHUR AND PRECEPT MINISTRIES INTERNATIONAL

KAY ARTHUR is known around the world as an international Bible teacher, author, conference speaker, and host of the national radio and television programs *Precepts for Life*, which reach a worldwide viewing audience of over ninety-four million. Recipient of the NRB Hall of Fame Award in 2011, Kay is a four-time Gold Medallion Award–winning author of more than one hundred books and Bible studies. She received an honorary doctorate from Tennesee Temple University.

Kay and her husband, Jack, founded Precept Ministries International in 1970 in Chattanooga, Tennessee, with a vision to establish people in God's Word. Today, the ministry has a worldwide outreach. In addition to inductive-study training workshops and thousands of small-group studies across America, PMI ministers in 180 countries with inductive Bible studies translated into more than seventy languages, discipling people by teaching them how to discover Truth for themselves.

Contact Precept Ministries International for more information about inductive Bible studies in your area.

Precept Ministries International
PO Box 182218
Chattanooga, TN 37422-7218
800-763-8280
www.precept.org

ABOUT BOB AND DIANE VEREEN

BOB AND DIANE VEREEN served for fifteen years as ambassadors-at-large for Precept Ministries International, overseeing a number of Precept's international offices. They both traveled the globe, speaking at conferences and teaching people how to study the Bible inductively as well as mentoring and training national leadership. They have been on staff since 1991, following sixteen years of prior involvement with Precept Ministries International. Bob was a contributor to *The New Inductive Study Bible* and has written for the New Inductive Study Series. He and Diane have coauthored several of the 40-minute Bible studies. Bob presently serves as the senior vice president of Precept International Ministries, and Diane serves as the director of outside published products and Precept's women's conferences.